D0802715

"Real life change begins with values—principles. When you have solid biblical principles, then you can live the worry-free life that God intended. That's what this book is all about. Apply what you read, and you'll immediately begin to sense some wind in your sails."

> —**Chris Hodges**, pastor, Church of the Highlands,
> Birmingham, Alabama; author of *Fresh Air*

"The rich young ruler in Luke 18:18–23 had everything, but when Jesus asked him to let go of his money, he couldn't; his wealth had a hold on him. We are called to take hold of our money, not let it take hold of us. We need the skills to steward our seed. In this book, Pastor John provides practical wisdom for everyday living to help you take hold of your financial world and make it one that brings forth great blessing and harvest. This book will bless and build you and is definitely a wise investment."

> —**Charlotte Gambill**, lead pastor, Life Church, England

"Wow—John Siebeling has hit the nail on the head in his book *Worry Free Finances*. Two of the biggest struggles that Christians and especially church leaders face are finances and worry. I might have to read this book once every year for the next few years and give a copy to all our staff. If you like Dave Ramsey—you will *love* John Siebeling and his teaching in *Worry Free Finances*."

> —**Philip Wagner**, lead pastor, Oasis Church, Los Angeles

WORRY
FREE
FINANCES

JOHN SIEBELING

BakerBooks
a division of Baker Publishing Group
Grand Rapids, Michigan

Published by Baker Books
a division of Baker Publishing Group
P.O. Box 6287, Grand Rapids, MI 49516-6287
www.bakerbooks.com

Printed in the United States of America

Library of Congress Cataloging-in-Publication Data is on file at the Library of
Congress, Washington, DC.

ISBN 978-0-8010-1506-9 (pbk.)

14 15 16 17 18 19 20   7 6 5 4 3 2 1

Contents

Introduction   7

Step 1 Tithe Consistently

1. Laying the Foundation for Worry-Free
   Finances   19
2. The Power of the First Part   29

Step 2 Manage Responsibly

3. Planning for Success   41
4. Developing Good Habits   53

Step 3 Build a Generous Spirit

5. The Foundation of a Generous Spirit   67
6. Blessed to Be a Blessing   77
7. The Secret of Contentment   89

Conclusion   99
Appendix: Budget Guide   103
Notes   105

Introduction

If you've ever worried about money, you're not alone. At some point or another, most of us have faced a stressful financial situation. Maybe you've encountered a serious financial issue that has caused you to carry an extremely heavy burden. Or maybe you aren't in the middle of a serious financial situation but you're still plagued by an underlying sense of worry, even when things are okay.

The origin of the word *worry* comes from the Old English word *wyrgan*, which means "to strangle or choke."[1] And that's exactly what worry does to us—it chokes much of the life out of us and leaves us merely surviving rather than thriving in life. It's hard to enjoy life when we're worried all the time. Unfortunately, for many people, finances and worry are inseparable. When we are trapped by worry, it's like we're being held prisoner. We aren't free to embrace the life God has called us to because we are limited and restrained by worry and fear. But that's not God's plan for our lives. And the good news is that he's given us a way to escape the grip of worry and walk in freedom. Jesus tells us in Luke 4:18–19:

The Spirit of the Lord is on me,
    because he has anointed me
    to proclaim good news to the poor.
He has sent me to proclaim freedom for the
        prisoners
    and recovery of sight for the blind,
to set the oppressed free,
    to proclaim the year of the Lord's favor.

The promise of true freedom might be the greatest promise for us as Christians. Think about how powerful that idea is—that we can live our lives not controlled by anything or anyone. It might seem impossible, but Jesus promises that freedom could and should be a part of following him. John 8:31–32 says, "If you hold to my teaching, you are really my disciples. Then you will know the truth, and the truth will set you free."

What does it mean to hold to Jesus's teachings? It means that we believe what he teaches in the Bible is truth and that we allow those principles to guide our lives. That truth is what can bring freedom if we choose to embrace it and live it.

As disciples of Jesus, not only do we have the opportunity to live in freedom, but it's actually our *responsibility* to live in freedom. It's not just a privilege or a benefit; it's a calling. The Bible tells us to live a life worthy of the calling we've received (Eph. 4:1). Part of "living worthy" is walking in freedom. Look again at John 8:31–32, and let's define the word *free* that Jesus uses. The original language of the New Testament was the Greek language. *The Expanded Vine's Expository Dictionary of New Testament*

Words defines the original word, *eleútheros*, as "free from bondage or slavery; freedom from restraint or obligation; freedom to go wherever one likes; free from sin; justified; liberty."[2]

Webster's New World College Dictionary defines *free* as "not imprisoned or enslaved; at liberty; not controlled by obligation or the will of another person."[3] Stop and think about that. Some people are literally controlled by other people. *Webster's* goes on to define free as "not affected or limited by specific conditions or circumstances."[4] In other words, a person who is free is not limited by anything, including their past mistakes.

The last part of the definition is awesome: "free from want; free of jealousy; to be uninhibited and outspoken; to be spontaneous; unconstrained; unconfined; not bound, fastened or attached."[5]

What an amazing picture that definition of freedom paints! That's a picture of the kind of life Jesus promises us. In the Bible, we see two ways we receive freedom into our lives.

Instant Freedom

This is the best kind of freedom, when we are instantly set free. This is what happens when we receive Christ. Our spirits are instantaneously set free, and we are forgiven and made clean. God touches our lives, and we experience an immediate change through God's power. When it comes to instant freedom, it seems the only requirement from us is faith, reaching out to God and believing. Specifically, in the area of salvation, our acceptance of God's gift is all that is required to receive the instant freedom that salvation offers.

There are other areas of life in which we may experience instant freedom, such as being healed physically, delivered from a stronghold such as addiction, or receiving emotional healing from past hurts. God is absolutely able to accomplish his work in our lives instantaneously, but it's important to know that instant freedom may not always happen. Sometimes God wants to work something in or out of us, and he chooses to free us through a process.

Progressive Freedom

Progressive freedom requires more from us because it's a process. Often God starts working in our hearts—maybe while reading the Bible, during an altar call, or through a sermon—and then it's a step-by-step process. It's like the pieces of a puzzle that start coming together one by one. We start with one piece, put it in place, and then God brings another piece, and we put that piece into place, building on what was already there. We make changes in our lives, and then we keep walking them out day by day. This is usually the way we begin walking in financial freedom. This kind of freedom takes some time, and it's something that comes into our lives progressively, rather than all at once.

Think about it. If we've spent our entire lives getting all tied up in knots, accepting Jesus and making a commitment to live for him won't necessarily mean that all the knots will miraculously come untied when we pray a salvation prayer or make a single decision to change a habit we've had for years. This kind of freedom doesn't always feel so spiritual while we're in the process. To be honest, it requires commitment and hard work. We have to start taking steps of obedience and faith as the Holy Spirit leads our lives forward.

I'm sure you've heard the story of the father who was trying to take a nap on the couch one Sunday afternoon while his little boy kept interrupting him with those famous words, "Daddy, I'm bored."

So the father, trying to make up a game, found a picture in the newspaper of a world map. He ripped it into a bunch of pieces and said, "Okay, here's a puzzle. I want you to put it all back together again."

He lay back down to finish his nap, thinking he would get at least another hour of sleep. In about fifteen minutes, the little boy woke him up, saying, "Daddy, I've got it finished. It's all put together."

He knew his son didn't know where all the nations went on the map, and so he was surprised to see it perfectly put together. He said, "How did you do that?"

The boy replied, "Dad, there was a picture of a person on the back, and when I got my person put together, the world looked just fine to me."

Our lives work much the same way. When we take obedient steps, one at a time, God helps us put the pieces of our lives together, and it's amazing how the world begins to look better. God does his part, and we have to do our part. We can't do God's part, and he will not do our part.

Remember the passage in John we looked at earlier? It said, "If you hold to my teaching . . . you will know the truth" (8:31–32). This speaks of responsibility. First, we have to find out the truth, but then we need to move on to holding and embracing it. We have to really know the truth for ourselves and take ownership of it. That means the truth changes how we live, how we think, and how we act. Just hearing the truth doesn't set us free. Hearing the truth and then applying that truth in our lives brings freedom. The Bible also says that when we hear the truth, faith comes. Romans 10:17 says, "Consequently, faith comes from hearing the message."

As we read God's Word and gain knowledge about his principles for handling finances, we increase our level of faith in God and his way of doing things. But even when faith is present, we still have to take a step. The step we take may require obedience, self-discipline, and determination. We have to *do* something!

Financial Freedom

There is no getting around the fact that many people are not walking in financial freedom. Think about these statistics:

- Experts tell us that 80 percent of Americans worry about money all the time.[6]

- Seventy percent of American households live from paycheck to paycheck, one unexpected situation away from financial collapse.[7]

- Consumer debt, mainly credit card debt, is nearing 2.8 trillion dollars.[8]

- There were 1.3 million bankruptcy filings in 2012.[9]
- Fifty-seven percent of American marriages end in divorce, with couples citing "financial problems as the primary reason for the demise of their marriage."[10]

These are not just statistics; they represent real-life stories. In our church, many weeks the most common prayer request is for God's help regarding a financial situation. I'm certain that if I took a poll and asked, "What do you worry about most?" the number one answer would be, "Money."

Doctors have long known that stress negatively affects our mental, emotional, and physical health—far more than most of us even realize. Sadly, the stress and worry of financial challenges often rob us of peace of mind, affect our health, and put us on edge emotionally. Many people are fighting the weight of these financial struggles year after year. No matter how much they want to, they just can't seem to break free from this cycle of financial bondage.

As I said before, God's plan is for us to walk in freedom, and that includes the financial arena of our lives. He doesn't want us to go through life constantly worried about financial issues and struggling to make ends meet. That's why the Bible addresses this important area of our lives over and over again. Think about this:

- Over two thousand Scriptures deal specifically with finances.
- The Bible addresses money more often than heaven and hell combined.

- Five times more is said about money than about prayer.
- Sixteen of the thirty-eight stories Jesus told deal with money management.

The Bible is packed full of sound financial advice and wisdom. If we want to break free from the grip of worry and walk in financial freedom, there's no better place to look than God's Word, the ultimate source of truth.

In this book, I want to look at and study three biblical principles that have the potential to change your life and your financial situation. These steps are like catalysts—they will bring freedom and momentum to your finances and peace to your mind as you commit to them and faithfully put them into practice. It's important to understand that they're interrelated and interdependent. In other words, you can't follow one and ignore the other two and expect God to bless your finances. You have to consistently apply yourself and put all three into practice to receive the blessings and benefits God wants you to experience. The three steps are:

1. Tithe consistently
2. Manage responsibly
3. Build a spirit of generosity

These concepts are so powerful because they are straight out of the Bible. Psalm 119:45 reminds us that God's ways bring freedom: "I will walk in freedom, for I have devoted myself to your commandments" (NLT).

Every principle in God's Word requires commitment from us. If we want God's best, we have to devote ourselves

14

to following his instructions. I encourage you to open your heart and mind to the truth of God's Word and to purpose in your heart to take the steps that are needed. As you receive God's truth and take practical steps, you'll experience his peace, his blessing, and his freedom in your life.

TITHE CONSISTENTLY

We can never learn too much of His will towards us, too much of His messages and His advice. The Bible is His word and its study gives at once the foundation for our faith and an inspiration to battle onward.

JOHN D. ROCKEFELLER

1

Laying the Foundation for Worry-Free Finances

In any project, the foundation is extremely important. It provides a secure starting point for future progress and lays the groundwork for long-term strength and success.

When we look to God's Word for his plan on handling our finances, we find a principle called "tithing." I believe that tithing is the first step we need to take and the foundation we need for walking in the freedom God wants us to experience in our finances. Tithing is a principle that's mentioned throughout the Bible, from Abraham in the Old Testament (Gen. 14:20) to Jesus in the New (Matt. 23:23). Tithing spans every era of God's plan for humans, and it's a principle we should make a part of our lives today.

Tithing

Depending on your background, you may not be familiar with the word *tithing*. Or maybe you've heard it, but you haven't received solid biblical teaching about it.

Let's start with a working definition of tithing and a foundational verse so we can begin to understand this principle.

Tithing is giving the first 10 percent of your income to God through your local church.

"Bring the whole tithe into the storehouse, that there may be food in my house. Test me in this," says the LORD Almighty, "and see if I will not throw open the floodgates of heaven and pour out so much blessing that there will not be room enough to store it." (Mal. 3:10)

For each of the three keys we will cover in this book, there is a "God principle" and "our commitment" that goes along with it. We partner with God in the process of becoming worry free in our finances. The first "God principle" is tithing. Our commitment is to consistently bring the first 10 percent of our income to God through our local church. Merriam-Webster defines the word *tithe* as "a tenth part of something."[1] The first part of Malachi 3:10 reads this way in the Amplified Version: "Bring all the tithes (the whole tenth of your income) into the storehouse."

If we are going to tithe according to biblical standards, our tithe will be 10 percent of our income. The amount we give as our tithe isn't up to us to decide. Many people haven't been taught this, so they are under the impression that the amount they tithe is up to them—and in that scenario, it's usually less than 10 percent. God makes it abundantly clear that we are to "bring the whole tithe." We could paraphrase it this way: "Bring the *whole* 10 percent; not just part of it."

God also tells us that the tithe is to be brought into the storehouse, which he also refers to as "my house" in Malachi 3:10. Throughout the Bible, God uses this phrase to refer to the temple, the place where his people gathered together to worship and to experience his presence. God's house or the temple refers to what we would today call our local church.

> Lord, I love the house where you live,
> the place where your glory dwells. (Ps. 26:8)

> And it came to pass, when the priests came out of the holy place, that the cloud filled the house of the Lord, so that the priests could not continue ministering because of the cloud; for the glory of the Lord filled the house of the Lord. (1 Kings 8:10–11 NKJV)

> He said to me: "Solomon your son is the one who will build my house." (1 Chron. 28:6)

When we bring our tithes to our local church, we help resource our church to do all that God has called it to do. Malachi 3:10 tells us that our tithe provides "food" for God's house. More than just the physical food or grains that would be brought to a literal storehouse, this "food" is really spiritual food that enables people to be nourished through the work of the church.

21

Notice that God says "bring," not "send." The tithe, the first part of our income, isn't something we send to a charity or a missionary. There is nothing wrong with giving to those kinds of things, and in fact, I encourage you to give to some of the many initiatives that are making a difference around the world. But those donations aren't a substitute for the tithe. According to the Bible, you should *bring* your tithe to the local church you are a part of. For some people, that creates a dilemma because they are not committed to a local church.

If that's you, then the first step for you is to find a church where you can put down roots and be "planted" or committed. Psalm 92:12–13 tells us, "The righteous will flourish like a palm tree, they will grow like a cedar of Lebanon; planted in the house of the LORD, they will flourish in the courts of our God." Being committed to a life-giving local church is a vital part of God's equation for living the abundant life Jesus talks about in John 10:10.

In the last part of Malachi 3:10, God encourages us to test him. He says that if we will bring the first 10 percent of our income to him through our local church, he will open the windows of heaven and bless our lives. God is serious about coming through for us if we do our part. But here's the thing: we go first.

A couple verses earlier in Malachi, God says, "Return to me, and I will return to you" (3:7). James 4:8 says, "Draw near to God and He will draw near to you" (NKJV). These verses show us that God responds to our initiative. He wants us to take the first step to move toward him. He wants to be close to us, but he doesn't force himself on us.

When we tithe, it's really a win-win situation. Our tithe provides for our local church, and God blesses our lives. Tithing isn't always easy, and it does require sacrifice, but God's instruction is clear: we need to bring the first 10 percent of our income to God through the local church we attend.

Here are a couple additional key thoughts about tithing.

Tithing Is Giving Back to God What Already Belongs to Him

Leviticus 27:30 says, "A tithe of everything from the land, whether grain from the soil or fruit from the trees, belongs to the LORD; it is holy to the LORD."

Our tithe, the first 10 percent of our income, actually *belongs* to God. It's not ours to keep and to do with as we please. If you told me you had figured out a way to get out of paying your taxes and keep that money for yourself, I'd do everything I could to convince you it wasn't a good idea. I'd say the same thing about choosing not to tithe. That first 10 percent of our income isn't ours—it's God's. It might seem harmless to keep it, but in the end, it isn't ever going to work out in your favor to keep what belongs to God. When we tithe, we aren't doing God a favor; we're simply returning to God what already belongs to him.

We have to change how we think about "our" money. Instead of thinking of it as ours to do with as we please, we have to retrain our minds (and our budgets) to see the first 10 percent as God's—not ours. The famous theologian Martin Luther is credited with saying, "There are three

23

conversions necessary: the conversion of the heart, the mind, and the purse."

What he meant was that when we are saved or come into a relationship with Jesus, a transformation needs to take place in our lives. Our hearts are changed, and we are cleansed of our sin and made right with God. But we also need to change how we think and how we handle our finances. You may not realize it, but if you fail to line up your life with God's Word in these two areas, you will limit your ability to experience life as God intended—to live a worry-free life.

When we are saved, our money gets saved too. That first 10 percent of our income becomes sacred, holy, set apart. We can't keep our old habits and our old ways of handling finances and fully embrace our transformed lives in Christ at the same time. We have to realign our views on finances so they line up with what God says in his Word. Ten percent belongs to God, and the other 90 percent is ours to manage.

Tithing Increases My Faith in God

Faith is an incredibly important part of our lives as believers. Hebrews 11:6 tells us, "And without faith it is impossible to please God, because anyone who comes to him must believe that he exists and that he rewards those who earnestly seek him."

Not only is faith essential for a healthy relationship with God, but it's also necessary for walking in financial freedom. Gaining freedom and overcoming worry start with believing that God has a good plan for our lives, including our finances. The first step to believing is faith.

Faith is what enables us to trust God enough to pursue him and follow his ways, even if it isn't always comfortable. Faith gives God room to move in a supernatural way in us. Being in control and doing things our own way doesn't require much faith. However, when we live this way, we're limited to "the natural"—what we can accomplish in our own strength.

When we live a life of faith, we tap into "the supernatural"—what God can do in his unlimited power and ability. God is capable of so much more than we are. When we put our faith in him, we open ourselves to exponentially more provision and blessing than we could ever experience on our own.

Part of living a life of faith means that we won't always have everything all figured out. It's going to require that we trust God to be true to his Word and come through for us, even when we don't see how. If we are reluctant to tithe, it stems from either a selfish desire to keep everything for ourselves or the fear that we won't have enough left to meet our needs. Both mentalities are rooted in a lack of trust in God and his promises.

It's important that we put faith into action when it comes to our finances. Practically speaking, this means trusting God enough to follow the principles he's given us in his Word. When we do, we are released to tithe confidently and joyfully. It's important to be responsible stewards of our finances, but sometimes we can use responsibility as an excuse to stay safe and not live by faith. If you're nervous about stepping out in faith and tithing, consider just a few of the benefits that faith brings into our lives:

- Faith changes our situations (Matt. 17:20; 21:21).
- Faith moves God to action (Matt. 9:2, 22; 15:28; Mark 2:5).
- Faith protects us (Eph. 6:16).
- Faith gives us confidence (Heb. 10:22; 11:1).
- Faith positions us to inherit God's promises for our lives (Heb. 6:12).

Faith has such a positive impact on our lives, and tithing is one of the most powerful steps of faith we can take. Some people think of tithing as a duty, but really it's an opportunity to take God at his Word and to see him work in our lives. Remember, God tells us to test him on this issue of tithing. I love how the Contemporary English Version puts it:

> I am the LORD All-Powerful, and I challenge you to put me to the test. Bring the entire ten percent into the storehouse, so there will be food in my house. Then I will open the windows of heaven and flood you with blessing after blessing. (Mal. 3:10)

God is issuing a challenge for us to put him to the test. Tithing requires faith, but when we do it, we will see for ourselves that God won't let us down. As a result, our faith will increase and we can take larger steps of faith. Choose to step out in faith in the area of tithing and give God a chance to come through for you.

When I'm facing a financial challenge, I have confidence when I pray and ask God to intervene and provide because I know I've done everything he has asked me to do. First John

3:21–22 says, "Dear friends, if our hearts do not condemn us, we have confidence before God and receive from him anything we ask, because we obey his commands and do what pleases him." Tithing is one of his commands, and as we obey and follow through with what he asks us to do, we can be sure that our confidence and faith in what God can do in our lives will increase.

The Best Investment You Can Make

Many people know Sir John Templeton as the billionaire founder of the Templeton Group of mutual funds. In 1999, *Money* magazine called him "arguably the greatest global stock picker of the century."[2] What many people don't know is that his faith played a significant role in his life and career. He was dedicated to a life of giving and helping others, and in 1987, he was knighted by Queen Elizabeth II for his philanthropic efforts.[3] Templeton is estimated to have given away over $1 billion over the course of his life.[4]

One reporter noticed a difference in how Templeton handled a profession often riddled with pressure and anxiety: "His unerring ability to stay calm as an investor is bolstered by his religious faith, which seems to free him from fears and doubts that paralyze others. Convinced he's a beloved child of God and that 'spiritual wealth is vastly more important than monetary wealth,' he's never been rattled by the market's plunges. Even when he took a beating, says Templeton, 'I never was depressed or despairing.'"[5]

Templeton called tithing the "single best investment" anyone can make.[6] He said, "Tithing always gives the greatest return on your investment."[7] He was committed to this principle in his own life, but he also advocated it in the lives of others as an essential ingredient for a happy and successful life. "I have observed 100,000 families over my years of investment counseling. I always saw greater prosperity and happiness among those families who tithed than among those who didn't."[8]

Tithing is part of God's prescription for managing our finances well. As we consistently put this core principle into action in our lives, we are laying the foundation for handling money God's way and experiencing freedom in our finances.

2

The Power of the First Part

As we look at this principle of tithing, it's important to remember that tithing is not just about money. It's so much more than dutifully setting aside the 10 percent we "owe" God so we can check it off our list and fulfill a religious obligation. It goes beyond money to something much deeper. The reason the Bible tells us to tithe is less about money and more about honoring God and giving him first place in our lives. Deuteronomy 14:23 tells us, "The purpose of tithing is to teach you always to put God first in your lives" (TLB).

Listen to what God said to his people in Malachi 3:7, right before he instructed them about tithing: "Return to me, and I will return to you." The people had wandered away from God. He wasn't a priority in their lives anymore. God wanted his people to be close to him, for their hearts to be turned toward him.

Our hearts and our finances are closely connected. Jesus tells us in Matthew 6:21, "Where your treasure is, there your heart will be also." How we handle our finances is an indication of our priorities and what's in our hearts.

Billy Graham once said, "Give me five minutes with a person's check book and I'll tell you where their heart is."[1] What God really wants from us is to have first place in our hearts.

First Things First

I mentioned in the last chapter that if we want to experience God's best for our lives, including our finances, we have to start by believing that God's plan for our lives is good. The first step to seeing that plan become a reality is faith. Now we're going to look at the second thing we are going to need: favor.

No matter how gifted we are, how well connected we are, or how good our plans are, our best efforts are not enough to take hold of God's best for our lives. We need something more—favor. I like to call favor "the God factor." Favor takes us beyond what we can do on our own and positions us to receive God's power working on our behalf to bring about his best for our lives.

But here's the thing. Favor isn't free. It doesn't just happen in our lives. It requires something from us. In studying favor in the Bible, I've found two things that bring favor into our lives: obedience and seeking God.

Obedience is simply doing what we've been asked to do with a willing heart. Obedience demonstrates to God that we love him and trust him. God looks favorably on people who obey the principles and instructions he gives us in his Word.

Seeking God means we are pursuing the things of God in our lives. We are open to his leading in the attitudes of our hearts and minds and in the direction of our lives. Seeking God is the opposite of being spiritually stagnant or complacent. Jeremiah 29:13 says, "You will seek me and find me when you seek me with all your heart." As we see in this verse, the kind of seeking God rewards is when we seek him with all our hearts.

If we're obedient to the instructions and principles God gives us in the Bible and *if* we are seeking God wholeheartedly and pursuing his will, *then* his favor will come into our lives. So many times we want favor without the effort of obeying and seeking God.

A timeless principle emerges in one of the earliest stories of the Bible about two brothers. Each presented an offering before God, but only one found favor with him.

"Now Abel kept flocks, and Cain worked the soil. In the course of time Cain brought some of the fruits of the soil as an offering to the LORD. And Abel also brought an offering—fat portions from some of the firstborn of his flock. The LORD looked with favor on Abel and his offering, but on Cain and his offering he did not look with favor" (Gen. 4:2–5).

These verses reveal that what we offer God affects the favor that flows back to us. God looked with favor on Abel and his offering, but he did not look with favor on Cain and his offering. Obviously, there was a crucial difference in the two offerings, but what was it?

31

At first glance, God's decision might not seem fair and even appear a little arbitrary. Cain and Abel both brought an offering; why was one acceptable and one not acceptable?

I believe the key is found in one little word in verse 4: *firstborn*. We're told that Abel brought "fat portions from some of the firstborn." Abel brought portions from the *firstborn* of his flock—the first part. Cain brought *some* portions, but they were not from the first crops of the soil. The firstborn was considered the best. Abel may not have known if there would be a second- or a thirdborn, but he gave the firstborn anyway. He wanted God to have his best. The powerful principle of the first part still applies to our lives today. When we give God our best, our first part, he releases his favor.

I love what Oswald Chambers says: "Worship is giving God the best that He has given you. Be careful what you do with the best you have. Whenever you get a blessing from God, give it back to Him as a love-gift. Take time to meditate before God and offer the blessing back to Him in a deliberate act of worship."[2]

We aren't bringing animals or produce from our fields to God to show our devotion today, but we do bring the first part of our income to God through our tithe. When we do, we're really performing an act of worship that shows our devotion to him. Here's what we have to remember: the favor is in the first part.

Leftovers

My wife is an amazing cook. When we have company over for dinner, I know there's going to be a feast. She puts a lot of thought into what she's going to serve. She plans the whole meal out, then goes to the grocery store with her list to do her shopping a few days ahead of time. Sometimes she cooks for several days to get ready for a big gathering. She goes all out to give our guests the best meal possible. She wouldn't dream of inviting company over for dinner and waiting until they arrive to dig through the refrigerator and pull out a random assortment of leftovers from last week's meals.

But all too often, that's what we do with God. We take care of our wants and needs, and when it's time to give, God ends up with the leftovers. After spending what we want and paying our bills, we scrape together what's left and offer it to God. Then we ask him to meet all our needs. If God is at the end of our priority list, how can we expect him to bless us?

When it comes to our finances, honoring God isn't so much about giving and giving and giving some more. It's about rearranging our priorities so that God is first in our lives. It's easy to say God is first, but does our spending reflect it? Usually our checkbook is a good place to find out our priorities. If we're serious about living for God, we've got to make him the number one priority in every area of our lives. In the same way, if we're serious about financial freedom, then we've got to make God the number one priority in our finances. When he's truly first in our lives, it's reflected in our finances.

By nature, we like to put ourselves first. We want to do things our way, on our time line, to achieve the result we want. Our natural, me-focused way of living doesn't line up with God's way of living, which causes a lot of headaches in our lives, especially in regard to our finances.

In his book *Master Your Money*, Ron Blue identifies the five things, in order, that most people do with their money.

1. Spend it
2. Pay bills/debt
3. Pay taxes
4. Save/invest it
5. Give it[3]

The issue isn't so much what we do with our money; it's the order in which we do it. It's a me-first list. As soon as we get paid, we've got a list a mile long of what we're going to do with that money. We've got it spent in our minds before we even get the check!

What we really need to do is take that me-first list and flip it upside down so it becomes a God-first list:

1. Give it
2. Save/invest it
3. Pay taxes
4. Pay bills/debt
5. Spend it

Matthew 6:33 says, "But seek first his kingdom and his righteousness, and all these things will be given to you as well." When God is first, he'll take care of everything else. Earlier in Matthew 6, God tells us not to worry about what we'll eat or what we'll wear. God knows exactly what we need, and he will provide for us when we put him first. It can be difficult for some people to believe this and really trust God to be their source. They're afraid they can't afford to tithe when in fact the opposite is true. I say we can't afford *not* to tithe. Putting God first is the only way to truly receive all God has for us. If we choose to ignore God's prescription for handling our finances, especially this foundational principle of tithing, we are stepping outside God's intended best for our lives.

Let's look at Malachi 3 again:

> "I the LORD do not change. So you, the descendants of Jacob, are not destroyed. Ever since the time of your ancestors you have turned away from my decrees and have not kept them. Return to me, and I will return to you," says the LORD Almighty. "But you ask, 'How are we to return?' Will a mere mortal rob God? Yet you rob me. But you ask, 'How are we robbing you?' In tithes and offerings. You are under a curse—your whole nation—because you are robbing me. Bring the whole tithe into the storehouse, that there may be food in my house. Test me in this," says the LORD Almighty, "and see if I will not throw open the floodgates of heaven and pour out so much blessing that there will not be room enough to store it." (vv. 6–10)

Showing our obedience by tithing and giving our first 10 percent positions us to receive God's favor and provision in our lives. But when we disobey by withholding our tithe, when we give God our leftovers—or worse, nothing at all—then we reap the consequences. In fact, God's Word goes so far as to call it a curse (Mal. 3:9). That's a loaded word for many people and may conjure up all kinds of images in your mind. But if you think about it, when you're stuck in place with your finances, it feels like you're cursed.

It's like being on a treadmill. You're constantly running and sweating, you're red-faced and worn-out, but you never actually get anywhere no matter what you do. Financially, the same thing can happen. You look at your life and realize that you're working hard, but you're still in the same place you were two years ago. Or worse, you're in more credit card debt, paying higher interest rates, and more stressed out than ever trying to pay your bills and keep your head above water. If that's not cursed, I don't know what is!

Jesus came to give us a full, overflowing life (John 10:10). His Word prescribes a way of living that positions us to receive and experience that life. We just have to believe him and put his principles into action in our lives. I don't know how it works, but 90 percent with God's blessing always works out better than 100 percent without it. I've seen it to be true in my own life and could share countless stories of others who've seen it in their lives too. The following is a testimony we received from an amazing couple who is now on staff at our church:

> "I would suggest that you seriously consider contacting a bankruptcy attorney." Never did we dream that we would hear these words from our accountant when we asked him to look over our financial records. Although these words were very hard to hear, we took full responsibility for the financial shape we found ourselves in. We were drowning in debt. The poor choices we had spent years making had finally caught up with us. We had lived a me-first life, giving little or no thought to how our choices and decisions were hindering our walk with God.

Fast-forward a couple of years. Still buried beneath the burden of debt, desperately trying to dig our way out, yet seeing no light at the end of the tunnel, we made a decision that would dramatically change our lives. One Sunday morning our family walked into the Life Church. From that divine moment on, our lives haven't been the same.

We will never forget the Sunday we heard the message on tithing. We'd never heard such solid, biblical teaching on this matter. We left that day determined to make tithing a priority in our family. We began to write the first check of the month to the Life Church. We realized we could no longer give God our leftovers.

We decided to place ourselves on a strict budget. For the first time in our lives, we desired to honor God with our finances. We felt a strong call to stewardship and began to attack our debt in a way we never had before. Literally, from the day we wrote our first check to the Life Church, God began to bless us. Our dental practice began to flourish. As other dental offices were suffering because of the hit the economy took in 2008, we were seeing more patients than ever before. That year our practice prospered above and beyond what we could have ever hoped. As we faithfully committed our first fruits to God, he faithfully provided for us. During 2008, we paid off $85,000 in debt.

Today, we are completely debt free. We paid off our mortgage, and we continue to live on a strict budget and faithfully offer our tithes and offerings to God. We are a living testimony of the principle of tithing. We have seen God's hand and experienced his blessings—not only financially but, much more importantly, spiritually. We are in awe of his greatness and amazed at his faithfulness.

This is just one of the many stories we've received from people who have seen firsthand what happens when they put God first and make tithing a priority in their lives. When God is first, we can be confident that he'll provide above and beyond what we could ever do on our own. I'm not saying it will always be easy or that it won't require some sacrifices on your part. But I am saying that it will be worth it because God's way is always the best way.

If you're already consistently tithing, keep it up. You're right on track. If this concept of tithing is completely new to you or if you haven't made it a regular practice in your life, I encourage you to take the next step and begin tithing consistently to your local church. The key word here is *consistently*. You can't tithe once and give up because you didn't see any change in your finances.

You must tithe faithfully if you want to see results. I'm confident that as you take this step and put this powerful principle of tithing into action, you'll see God move and you will begin to gain momentum in your finances.

MANAGE
RESPONSIBLY

*It takes as much energy
to wish as it does to plan.*

ELEANOR ROOSEVELT

3

Planning for Success

After laying a solid foundation by tithing consistently, the second step we must take if we want financial freedom is to become responsible managers of what God has given us. Another word we could use for this is *stewardship*. This simply means managing something that belongs to someone else.

Managing our money wisely can be quite a challenge at times. God's Word serves as an incredible resource to help us succeed in this area of our lives. Let's take a look at some practical insights from the Bible on what it means to be a responsible manager.

Ownership versus Stewardship

One of the most important truths we have to work out in our hearts and minds is that everything we own really belongs to God—because we belong to God. First Corinthians 6:19–20 tells us, "You are not your own; you were bought at a price." We are God's, and everything we have has been given to us by him. When we realize this, it changes our perspective on money, our possessions, and our role in managing them.

James 1:17 says, "Every good and perfect gift is from above, coming down from the Father." And Psalm 24:1 says, "The earth is the LORD's, and everything in it, the world, and all who live in it." We are not the *owners*; we are simply the *managers*. That means that "our stuff" isn't really our stuff at all; it's God's! We have a responsibility to manage our finances in a way that pleases God because anything we have is a gift from him. The second "God principle" is stewardship. Our commitment is to be responsible managers of the money God gives us.

First Corinthians 4:2 says, "Now, a person who is put in charge as a manager must be faithful" (NLT). The Amplified Version says, "Worthy of trust." One quality of good managers is that they can be trusted to make good decisions with the things they have been entrusted with. A stewardship mentality sees our money, however much or little we have, as God's resource poured out into our lives for the purpose of meeting our needs, blessing us, and accomplishing his purposes in the world through us. Good stewards feel a sense of responsibility to please God, rather than just themselves, when it comes to managing money.

It's important that we understand the relationship between tithing and being a responsible manager of our money. These two principles are *interrelated* and *interdependent*, meaning they work together and depend on each other to function properly. We can't follow one but not the other and expect God to bless our finances. We've got to obey God by tithing the first 10 percent of our income *and* by being responsible managers of our finances.

Think of it in terms of weight loss and physical fitness. If you're trying to lose weight, you can't run for ten minutes, then eat Krispy Kreme doughnuts for breakfast, a McDonald's quarter pounder with cheese for lunch, and a large meat lover's pizza from Pizza Hut for dinner and wonder why you're not losing weight. It just doesn't work that way!

That kind of logic doesn't work for our finances either. Even after giving God first place and faithfully tithing, we can't sit back and continue our bad habits, waiting for God to whisk away the financial mess our bad habits have created. We have to commit and be faithful to tithe and then do our part to manage the remaining 90 percent of our income wisely.

As with tithing, being a good manager is straight from God's Word. But understanding God's principles usually isn't the hard part. Walking them out is more challenging. If we want to experience God's blessings in our lives, we have to be willing to change our ways and put his principles into action. Oftentimes, we lock into the promise and the blessing, but we resist the process it takes to achieve them. I meet so many people who know the right thing to do, but they're having a hard time taking the steps needed to actually do it. We only see the blessing when we hold on to the promise *and* commit to the process.

If this sounds difficult or intimidating to you or you've struggled with managing money in the past, I want you to know that it *is* possible for you to be a wise manager of your finances. You don't need to have an accounting degree to manage your finances successfully. The truth is that "personal finance" is really more personal than it is financial. It's 20 percent head knowledge and 80 percent behavior. Being a responsible manager is largely about managing ourselves—having discipline and using wisdom to make decisions about the money we have.

Proverbs 21:5 says, "Good planning and hard work lead to prosperity, but hasty shortcuts lead to poverty" (NLT). We have to plan well and be willing to work hard. If we do those two things consistently, they will yield great benefits.

Let's unpack some action steps in this area of stewardship. Here are two practical ways to incorporate good planning into your finances:

1. Define your financial goals
2. Design a working budget

Define Your Financial Goals

When faced with a challenging financial situation, many people want to focus on the immediate problem. While that's important, we can't just fix our present situation; we also need to change our future. We need to start by identifying what we want our future to look like. As Zig Ziglar puts it, "If you aim at nothing, you will hit it every time."[1]

I am a huge advocate of setting goals. Goals give us something to reach for and make it easier to pay the price now for what we want to accomplish later. It's good to be specific when we do this. "I want to reduce my debt by 20 percent by this time next year" is much better than "I want less debt" because it gives us some accountability and helps us put together a plan to make it happen. It's also a great idea to write down goals and revisit them often.

Here are some simple goals that should be a priority when it comes to our finances.

- Tithe and give
- Save and invest
- Eliminate debt

Tithe and Give

We have already talked about tithing in depth, but let me remind you that tithing is an act of obedience to God. It shows God that he has first place in our lives and positions us to receive his favor and blessing. The first step to truly experiencing financial freedom is to get God involved in our finances. Tithing opens the door for God to start moving in our financial lives. When we tithe, not only are we positioning ourselves for God's favor, but we are also having an eternal impact on God's kingdom through our local church.

Save and Invest

Saving is so simple, and yet so many of us fail to do it. The average American spends more than he or she makes. Many people can't even cover their expenses each month, let alone save. In our shortsighted society, we've placed more value on getting what we want now than using wisdom and planning for the future.

45

Proverbs 21:20 says, "The wise man saves for the future, but the foolish man spends whatever he gets"(TLB). The Bible is very straightforward. If you spend everything you make and don't save anything, you're a fool. The word *fool* in Proverbs refers to an immoral, immature person. We see throughout the book of Proverbs that foolishness carries serious consequences. On the other hand, the Bible says that if you save, you're wise and will reap great benefits.

Here are three basic reasons we should save:

1. Saving keeps us focused and disciplined.
2. Saving brings a sense of peace and security.
3. Saving creates a reserve fund for emergencies.

Let's focus on that last one for a minute. The average American doesn't have access to one thousand dollars in cash.[2] That means when an emergency arises, we are forced to depend on credit. This is why many Americans find themselves in trouble financially. Many people are only one emergency away from financial disaster. Part of being a responsible manager is being wise and saving so that we're financially prepared for whatever comes our way. Start saving now, even if it's only five dollars a week. No matter how bad your financial picture looks, find a way to begin saving something.

Some people will say, "Debt is causing me the most trouble; wouldn't it be better just to focus on that before I start tithing and saving?" The answer is no for many reasons, but here are two of the most important ones.

First, when we tithe, we are being obedient to God's Word. Giving God first place in our finances opens the door for him to be involved and positions us to receive God's blessings. Disobedience in the area of tithing blocks God's blessings from flowing into our lives.

Second, both tithing and saving are habits. One of the main reasons people find themselves in financial trouble is that they haven't developed good habits. To experience financial freedom, it's essential that we immediately change how we do things and begin to establish good habits. If you keep doing what you've always done, you'll keep getting what you've always gotten. Different results require different habits.

Eliminate Debt

Romans 13:8 says, "Keep out of debt and owe no man anything, except to love one another" (AMP). Debt is one of the most crippling, devastating problems people in our nation face today. According to the US Census Bureau, the average American spends $1.33 for every $1.00 he or she earns.[3] That means that on average such people are spending 33 percent more than they make. Credit cards have allowed us to spend money we don't have, and for many people, credit has created a problem that's taking over their lives.

Think about how quickly debt can get out of control. If you make $40,000 a year and overspend by 10 percent in a year, you owe $4,000 on credit cards. You think, "No big deal. I'll pay it off next year when I get that raise." But the overspending continues, and five years later, you have $20,000 in credit card debt. Add on to that an extremely high interest rate, and it's going to take you forty years to pay off the balance if you make only minimum payments.

Proverbs 22:7 says, "The rich rule over the poor, and the borrower is slave to the lender." Notice the two key words *rule* and *slave*. Both of them are used negatively and indicate bondage. When we are in debt, we become a slave to that debt. It begins to rule our lives. We are no longer calling the shots. We are being ruled by money, other people, circumstances, and what we don't have. The Bible says we should be ruled and controlled only by Christ. The reality is that many of us are controlled by our money, or lack thereof, and therefore are in bondage. God doesn't want us to be bound by anything. That's why it's so important that we begin to eliminate debt and escape its hold on our lives.

Of those people who declare bankruptcy, 53 percent do so because of credit card debt.[4] There is a credit epidemic in our society today. It's so easy to get what we want or "need" without having to feel the weight of what it will cost us. American culture has adopted a mentality that demands instant gratification. We've got to resist that mentality if we are going to be financially free.

In his book *Financial Peace*, Dave Ramsey offers basic guidelines for how much people should give, save, and use to reduce debt:

Giving: 10–15 percent of income

Saving: 5–10 percent of income

Debt reduction: 5–10 percent of income[5]

Of course, we can have other goals, but these guidelines give us a place to begin.

In addition, there are two important questions we must ask ourselves when it comes to goals:

1. *What is my goal?* Write it down and be specific. Look at it often.
2. *What do I need to do to get there?* Outline some action steps you can start doing right now.

Design a Working Budget

Proverbs 27:23 says, "Be sure you know the condition of your flocks, give careful attention to your herds." This verse tells us that we're responsible for knowing the status and condition of what we've been given to manage. Otherwise, we won't be able to make good decisions. A budget is simply a tool that helps us get a look at our financial situation. If you don't use one, you must start. It's a basic requirement for good stewardship and financial success. We can't expect God to bring increase and trust us with more if we're not successfully managing what we've been given. If we want to live in financial freedom, we must live within our means. There's just no way around it. A budget is an essential tool.

Here are some practical tips for designing a successful budget.

Find Out Where Your Money Is Going

Take ninety days and document everything you spend. This will help you understand where your money is really going. You may think you don't have time to do this, but if you have time to worry about money, you have time to keep a simple log. There are many ways you can do this—using a program on your computer, an app on your phone, or just an old-fashioned pencil and paper list. Find what works best for you. When you know where you're spending your money, you can manage it better. You may need to cut out premium cable or take your daily Starbucks down to once a week. I'm not saying it's easy, but the rewards of living within your means far outweigh the pain of a little self-denial.

Plan Your Budget Each Month

You may have heard the saying, "If your outgo exceeds your income then your upkeep becomes your downfall." Having a budget simply means telling our money where to go instead of wondering where it went.

Your ninety-day record will show a number of fixed and variable expenses that come up each month. You also have a certain amount of income each month with which to pay those expenses. If the total of your expenses is more than you bring in each month, you're going to be in trouble and will need to make some adjustments. If you don't have a detailed list of your expenses, you are flying blind. Housing and automobiles are the two biggest areas where people tend to overspend and get into trouble. I encourage you to look at the simple budget guide at the end of this book will help you list your expenses and identify any areas you need to adjust.

Evaluate and Adjust Each Month

Make it a priority to set aside time each month to work on your budget (with your spouse if you're married). Start by reviewing the previous month. Then talk about the coming month so you can account for any upcoming expenses or make changes in areas that need adjustment. If the bottom line is negative, redo your budget until you have a plan that works.

Remember Proverbs 21:5: "Good planning and hard work lead to prosperity, but hasty shortcuts lead to poverty" (NLT). Planning and preparation are part of being a good manager. They won't necessarily change our financial picture immediately, but they will help us assess where we are now, get a vision for the future, and establish some action steps for how to achieve it. But even the best plan is powerless if we don't work the plan. That's where hard work comes in. Financial freedom requires something on our part. It may not always be easy, but it will pay off.

Having a plan is a great antidote for worry. When we pair our planning with hard work, they will bring a significant sense of order and peace to this area of our lives.

4

Developing Good Habits

As we look at what it takes to manage our finances with wisdom, it's important that we recognize the role our inner life plays—our individual habits, tendencies, mind-sets, and even character. As we said before, personal finance is mostly personal. For many people, habits or character issues may be hindering them from making progress in the financial arena of their lives. I've seen a single bad habit or character issue cause tremendous damage to someone's finances.

We can tithe and even set up a budget, but if we don't also develop good habits and strong character, we will not have long-term success. Good habits can be powerful forces in our lives, creating long-term, positive effects.

Conversely, bad habits can keep us from moving forward, producing destructive results.

I want to challenge you to look at anything in your life that may be hindering you from being a responsible manager. Whatever those things may be, make the choice to deal with them and to develop good habits to carry you forward.

Think back to Proverbs 21:5: "Good planning and hard work lead to prosperity, but hasty shortcuts lead to poverty" (NLT). We talked about good planning in the last chapter. But we can't put together a great plan for budgeting and debt reduction and then let bad habits sabotage our plan. Bad habits have a way of sneaking up on us, whether it's using our "emergency credit card" for things we don't really need, eating out too much, or not taking the time to track our spending.

Getting rid of our bad habits and developing good ones isn't always easy. I know this firsthand. When I find something I enjoy, whether it's a hobby, a gadget, or a certain drink at Starbucks, it can be easy for me to slip into a bad habit of overindulgence. But when it comes to trying to develop new, positive habits, such as working out and changing my eating habits, it takes a lot more work and discipline. But the more I do them, the easier they become. I just have to stick with them until they become part of my new normal.

It can be the same way with our finances. Building good financial habits requires time, patience, consistency, accountability, and lots of effort (aka hard work!). But it's worth it. When you change a habit, your hard work pays off significantly in the long run. You don't have to continue fighting the same battle over and over.

Here are two things we need to do if we want to establish good habits, especially when it comes to managing our finances.

Identify Poor Habits and Underlying Mind-sets

Lasting change comes when we adjust the way we think. Our actions are a result of our thoughts, which reflect our values, perspectives, and mentalities. If we want to have lasting change in our behavior, we can't just try to adjust our actions. We have to press deeper and address the underlying thinking patterns and mentalities that cause that behavior.

When Leslie and I were first married, we had a lot of debt. I didn't know much at all about how to manage finances. The concept of budgeting was the farthest thing from my mind. The way I grew up, if you wanted something, you bought it. If you couldn't afford to pay for it with cash, you just put it on a credit card. To me, a credit card gave me the "freedom" I wanted in my finances. But no one told me how quickly those charges add up and how deadly the interest rates are. My finances were a mess!

Finally, I got fed up with being in debt. We asked God to help us get out of debt, and we worked hard to pay it off. And we did, which was pretty incredible, considering how much debt we had. But then I slipped back into my old habits. Before I knew it, we were right back in debt again, this time worse than before.

I knew something had to change, so I prayed again that God would help us get out of debt. But much to my disappointment, nothing changed overnight as I had hoped.

Then I started looking at our situation from God's perspective, learning what he had to say about money in his Word. As I did, my way of thinking about money began to change.

I began making different and better choices, and those better choices eventually turned into better habits, and those better habits helped us get out of debt. It was a gradual transition. I wanted God to change the problem, but he wanted to change me. That was what I really needed to live in sustained freedom for the long-term.

We are constantly bombarded with messages about money and spending that aren't going to steer us toward God's best. Some people approach money with a poverty mentality because that's what they learned from their family. Others have an entitlement mentality that says, "I deserve this, so I'm buying it, even if I can't afford it." The media tells us we deserve nice things, so we justify spending more than we should on things we want. Instead of basing our foundational principles for money management on what everyone else is doing, we have to base them on the principles of wisdom and truth in God's Word.

Romans 12:2 says, "Do not conform to the pattern of this world, but be transformed by the renewing of your mind." If we want our financial picture to change, we have to change the way we think about money. Training our minds to have a healthy, Bible-based mentality about money is one of the most important things we can do on our journey to walking in financial freedom

Lasting change in our habits comes when we change not only our actions but also our thinking patterns. As our thoughts and habits change, we are in a position to achieve and maintain long-term health and strength in our finances.

Develop Strong Character

God's principles always work together to fulfill his promises in our lives, so it's important that we work to make sure our lives, as a whole, are in line with God's Word. The Bible talks a lot about the character qualities we should develop. We should make the pursuit of these qualities a priority simply because the Bible teaches us to do so. But a natural by-product of these character qualities is that they also position us for success. Strong, godly character never goes unrewarded by God.

I want to highlight three key character qualities that can bring significant momentum into our lives and our finances.

1. Discipline
2. Diligence
3. Faithfulness

We are responsible for developing these qualities in our lives. They won't develop on their own, and no one else can develop them for us. They are essential qualities we must understand and practice if we want freedom and success in our finances, or in any other area of our lives.

Discipline

Have you ever known someone who had a lot of potential but just couldn't seem to get it together? I've known many people who had so much going for them, but they never lived up to their potential because they weren't disciplined. They didn't have self-control. They just couldn't bring themselves to control their desires and do what they needed to do rather than what they wanted to do.

This is one of the biggest challenges we face when it comes to handling our finances and being responsible managers. Our desires are so strong, and we're constantly faced with messages urging us to give in and indulge ourselves in whatever we want. Sometimes we need to do exactly the opposite. We need to have the strength to reign in our desires and live with wisdom and a vision for the future.

Proverbs 10:17 says, "The road to life is a disciplined life" (Message). And Proverbs 5:23 says, "Death is the reward of an undisciplined life; your foolish decisions trap you in a dead end" (Message). That may sound harsh, but it's true. Discipline leads us to good things—being in shape, good health, a secure financial picture, and strong relationships. Lack of discipline produces the opposite.

I think discipline, or self-control, is one of the most foundational character traits that affect our finances. The best budget in the world won't do us any good if we can't find the self-control to stick to it. If we want God's best, we can't be ruled by our impulses, feelings, or desires. You may have heard the saying, "Don't give up what you want most for what you want now." We've got to keep the big picture in mind, take responsibility for our actions, and do what it takes to keep ourselves on track.

Diligence

Proverbs 27:23 says, "Be diligent to know the state of your flocks, and attend to your herds" (NKJV). *Diligence* may not be a word we hear often today, but I believe it is one of the greatest character traits we can possess. It's a common quality among highly successful people.

Diligence can be defined as "giving the degree of care required in a given situation; a persevering determination to perform a task,"[1] "the opposite of negligence."[2] The original Latin word that *diligence* is derived from, *diligere*, meant "to value highly; to love, esteem, prize; to choose."[3]

Diligence is not just *hard* work. It is *heart* work—choosing to put your heart and energy into seeing a project completed well.

In Proverbs, we see that diligence brings great benefits into our lives.

1. *Promotion*. This is the gaining of influence. "Work hard and become a leader; be lazy and become a slave" (Prov. 12:24 NLT).

2. *Wealth*. This is achieving or earning an abundant supply of resources: not just monetary wealth and resources but wealth in our reputation, ability, character, wisdom, and experience. "Lazy hands make for poverty, but diligent hands bring wealth" (Prov. 10:4).

3. *Satisfaction*. This is the contentment found in having our desires fulfilled and needs met. "A sluggard's appetite is never filled, but the desires of the diligent are fully satisfied" (Prov. 13:4).

4. *Profit*. This is being in a position of receiving more than we put in and having a valuable return for our effort. "The plans of the diligent lead to profit as surely as haste leads to poverty" (Prov. 21:5).

I've found that diligent people share five characteristics. These are not gifts some people are born with or qualities that only a few of us can attain. Instead, these characteristics are based on choices people make to live a certain way and to be relentless in their commitment to this way of life.

1. *Diligent people work hard.* Too many people have an aversion to hard work and are always looking for ways to get out of it. You can't show up late, cut out early, and do a shoddy job and still expect your boss to give you a raise. Life just doesn't work that way.

2. *Diligent people don't give up easily.* In the face of resistance, challenges, even failure, diligent people keep pressing on. Thomas Edison experienced thousands of failed attempts at creating a light bulb. He kept trying until he found a solution that worked.

3. *Diligent people go the extra mile.* They are committed to excellence, even if it's inconvenient and requires extra effort. They aren't satisfied with doing an okay job. They go above and beyond to give their best.

4. *Diligent people are committed to follow through.* Unfortunately, many people have good ideas and intentions, but they fail to follow through on them. At the end of the day, good intentions don't get us far. Diligent people are good finishers—they take the necessary steps to see their plans through to completion.

5. *Diligent people know that details matter.* They aren't concerned with doing a task "mostly right." They want to make sure it's done correctly and done well, down to the last detail.

If you've ever typed a word on your phone and had autocorrect change it, you know how much just one word—or even one letter for that matter—can change the meaning of your message. One "insignificant" detail could get you into a lot of trouble!

UCLA basketball coach John Wooden was known for being a stickler about details. At the beginning of each season, he would show his players a very specific way to put their socks on so there were no wrinkles in them. His reason was twofold. First, wrinkles resulted in blisters, and blisters impaired performance. Impaired performance cost games. Second, he wanted his players to understand that even the smallest, seemingly unimportant detail could impact their ultimate success. He firmly believed that "details create success."[4] Wooden drove into his players the importance of "the little things" because, as he said, "It's the little details that are vital. Little things make big things happen."[5] Diligence is a character trait that creates success in our lives.

Work hard, put your whole heart into a task, and be willing to go the extra mile. Do a great job at whatever you do, and you'll be rewarded—not just by men but by God. Diligence is a quality God rewards. Colossians 3:23–24 says, "Whatever you do, work at it with all your heart, as working for the Lord, not for human masters, since you know that you will receive an inheritance from the Lord as a reward. It is the Lord Christ you are serving."

Faithfulness

First Samuel 26:23 tells us, "The LORD rewards everyone for their righteousness and faithfulness." There are rewards associated with faithfulness, both tangible and intangible. When we're faithful, people can trust us without reservation. We can be counted on.

When it comes to our finances, we've got to be faithful with what we have if we want God to bless us with more. We need to prove that God can trust us with what he's given us.

First Corinthians 4:2 says, "Now it is required that those who have been given a trust must prove faithful." Notice it says "must." This isn't an option or a suggestion. God *requires* us to be faithful with the things he's given us. Earlier we talked about the fact that everything we have is really God's and that we are simply managers. It doesn't matter how much or how little we have. If we have been given anything, we are automatically in a position that requires us to be faithful with it.

You may think you don't have much to be faithful with or to manage. Let me ask you this: What are you doing with what you *do* have? Are you managing it well? Are you making wise decisions concerning it? Are you taking care of the money, the car, the job God has blessed you with? If you aren't doing a good job managing what you do have, God probably isn't going to give you more to mismanage.

Faithfulness is a key to increase, advancement, and promotion. When we are faithful with what is in our hands, we position ourselves for God to bless us with more. Matthew 25:23 says, "Well done, my good and faithful servant. You have been faithful in handling this small amount, so now I will give you many more responsibilities. Let's celebrate together!" (NLT).

Matthew Easton's *Illustrated Bible Dictionary* tells us that when the word *faithful* is used "as a designation of

Christians, it means full of faith, trustful, and not simply trustworthy."[6] As we talked about earlier, faith is essential if we want to live a life that's pleasing to God and moving forward in freedom. Part of being faithful in managing our finances is choosing to live full of faith, not full of doubt and fear.

God passionately loves us and wants to take care of us. To be worry free, we must fully release our hearts to believe that God's principles are true and that he can be trusted. Even if we are in the middle of difficult circumstances, his plans for us are good, and he holds a bright future (Jer. 29:11–13).

There's no better plan for success than following the principles found in the Bible. When we develop good habits, keep our thinking in line with God's Word, and develop our character, we position ourselves to experience the fullness of God's promises in our lives and finances.

BUILD A GENEROUS SPIRIT

You can always give without loving, but you can never love without giving.

Amy Carmichael

5

The Foundation of a Generous Spirit

The third step we need to take to live in financial freedom is to build a generous spirit. We can tithe and manage our finances wisely, but without generosity, we're missing a major part of the equation. If we're going to follow God's prescription for handling money, a generous spirit is essential.

Generosity is a principle found in God's Word, and it works together with the principles of stewardship and tithing. Together, these three help us manage our finances in a way that honors God and positions us to live worry free. The third "God principle" is generosity. Our commitment is to make sure we build a generous spirit in our hearts and minds. For many people, this is the missing link in their approach to finances.

Let's look at the definition of both *generous* and *spirit* and then identify some key thoughts from the Bible about having a generous spirit.

Generous is defined as "willing to give and share; not petty or small in character and mind;[1] openhanded."[2] One of the definitions Merriam-Webster gives for the word *spirit* as "the activating or essential principle influencing a person; an inclination, impulse, or tendency of a specified kind; a special attitude or frame of mind; the feeling, quality, or disposition characterizing something."[3]

Having a generous spirit isn't just about giving away large sums of money. A willingness to freely give of our resources is part of it, but being generous is really more about the spirit we carry within us, the attitude of our hearts and minds. It's choosing to live openhanded rather than tightfisted. It spans the breadth of our lives and impacts every area. A generous spirit is important to financial freedom, but more importantly, it's a mark of a healthy Christian who's living according to God's Word.

Generosity should be not only a core value that influences *what we do* but also a defining characteristic of *who we are*. Having a generous spirit goes deeper than our actions. Proverbs 23:6–8 shows us that we can actually have generous actions without having a generous heart or spirit: "Do not eat the bread of a miser, nor desire his delicacies; for as he thinks in his heart, so is he. 'Eat and drink!' he says to you, but his heart is not with you. The morsel you have eaten, you will vomit up, and waste your pleasant words" (NKJV).

Generous actions that don't flow from a generous heart aren't pleasing to God or the people we direct them toward. True generosity is determined by the condition of the heart.

That's why it's important that we go beyond simply committing to acts of generosity and instead commit to developing a heartfelt spirit of generosity in our lives.

Why Should We Cultivate a Generous Spirit?

The Bible Tells Us To

First Timothy 6:18 says, "Command them to do good, to be rich in good deeds, and to be generous and willing to share." Simply put, the primary reason we should be generous is that the Bible tells us to. This is a theme we see throughout the Bible. In the Old Testament, God commands his people to be generous to those who are less fortunate (Deut. 15). The books of Psalms and Proverbs share with us the benefits for those who are generous, especially to the poor (see Ps. 37:26; 112:5; 19:7; Prov. 11:24–26; 19:17; 22:9). In the New Testament, Paul constantly encourages believers to be generous, reminding them of the importance of their generosity (see 2 Cor. 8:10–15; 9:6–15; 1 Tim. 6:17–19; Phil. 4:15–20). Generosity is, and always has been, a part of God's plan for his people.

In the Bible, the word *believe* is used 408 times, *pray* 438 times, *love* 763 times, and *give* 1,729 times. As you can see, the word *give* is used more than twice as many times as *love*.[4] Clearly, giving is important to God, and it should be important to us too.

Psalm 37:21 tells us, "The wicked borrow and do not repay, but *the righteous give generously*" (emphasis mine). Here we see that righteousness and giving generously go hand in hand; they are inseparable. "The righteous" refers to those people who choose God's ways. If we are Christians who are choosing God's ways, generosity isn't really an option. It's part of how God expects all believers to live.

Generosity Is the Essence of Godliness

John 3:16 says, "For God so loved the world that he gave his one and only Son, that whoever believes in him shall not perish but have eternal life." God loved us, so he *gave*. And not just anything. He gave what was most precious to him. As believers, we are created in God's image and called to be like Christ. Jesus gave his very life for us; he didn't hold anything back. If we are going to be like him, we're going to be willing to give, even things that are precious to us.

We can't be stingy and Christlike at the same time. Those two things can't coexist. As Christians, we should be the most giving people on the planet because God has been so gracious and generous toward us. And his generosity toward us wasn't a one-time thing. It continues to flow toward us in every way. "He who did not spare his own Son, but gave him up for us all—how will he not also, along with him, graciously give us all things?" (Rom. 8:32). There is nothing stingy about God.

Psalm 84:11 tells us, "The LORD will withhold no good thing from those who do what is right" (NLT). God's attitude toward us is generous and openhanded. Building a generous spirit is one of the most significant ways we can be like him.

A Generous Spirit Expands Our World

Living with a generous spirit brings a multitude of personal benefits into our lives. It's important to understand that generosity is something we commit to simply because it is in the Word of God. We obey God's principles, whether they benefit our lives or not, but the truth is that when we live with a generous spirit, good things come into our lives.

Studies show that the one who benefits the most from generosity is the person who is being generous.[5] This is exactly what God's Word tells us too. Proverbs 11:17 says, "The merciful, kind, and generous man benefits himself [for his deeds return to bless him], but he who is cruel and callous [to the wants of others] brings on himself retribution" (AMP). When we have compassion and are moved to act generously on someone else's behalf, we're sowing good seeds that cause good things to grow in our lives. But the opposite is true as well. We determine what flows back to us by what flows out from us.

What I've found is that generosity is like a catalyst. It initiates change and brings momentum into our lives. It stirs up the work of the Holy Spirit and causes God to move on our behalf. Proverbs 11:24 says, "The world of the generous gets larger and larger; the world of the stingy gets smaller and smaller" (Message). This verse refers to both tangible and intangible things. It's telling us that a generous spirit brings expansion and favor into every area of our lives.

I'm so thankful for the people who are in my world and the relationships I have. I think about the opportunities God has given me and Leslie and the doors he has opened over the years. Many of those things were birthed out of a moment of generosity. Our lives have been enriched and our world expanded because we made the commitment to live with a generous spirit.

We often describe our life as our "circumstances." If you look at the word *circumstance*, it's a combination of two words, *circum*, which means "circle or round," and *stance*, which means "to stand." So we can picture our world, or our circumstances, as a circle in which we stand. If we are hoping and believing for big things—meaning we have some goals and dreams for progress and expansion in our lives—we have to realize that expansion in our world comes when we live with a generous spirit. As generosity flows from our lives, more freedom, more favor, more blessings, and more opportunities flow back into our lives. This God principle causes the boundaries of our lives to expand.

Conversely, the world of the stingy gets smaller and smaller. If you're feeling frustrated and confined by your circumstances, it could be that you've been tightfisted and stingy instead of openhanded and generous. Most people who are tightfisted live in a place of fear. What they don't realize is that fear actually causes their world to close in on them. Faith and fear are opposites. Fear causes us to cling tightly to what we have. Faith enables us to willingly share what we have, knowing God will honor our generosity.

A seed you sow always produces more than if you keep it for yourself. Think about a farmer. He can do two things with his seed: plant it or consume it. If he chooses to use it for food, once that meal is done, he's reached the end of his return from that seed. But if he chooses to plant it, he'll get far more in return than what he started with. Generosity acts the same way in our lives. What we give goes on to produce far more than we could ever create if we choose to keep it for ourselves.

Key Ingredients of a Generous Spirit

If you want to have a generous spirit, a few key elements must be present in your life.

Faith

Philemon 1:6 says, "You are generous because of your faith. And I am praying that you will really put your generosity to work, for in so doing you will come to an understanding of all the good things we can do for Christ" (NLT). Let's focus on the first part of that verse: "You are generous *because of your faith*" (emphasis mine). The first thing we need in order to have a generous spirit is faith. Clearly, when faith is present in our lives, it produces generosity. Faith helps free us from fear so we can act according to God's instructions. True faith moves us to action. In fact, without action, faith is not really faith at all (James 2:17). Faith doesn't mean we have everything figured out or we don't have any concerns, but it does mean we choose to follow God's Word over our feelings. First Timothy 6:17 says, "Teach those who are rich in this world not to be proud and not to trust in their money, which is so unreliable. Their trust should be in God, who richly gives us all we need for our enjoyment" (NLT).

When we truly believe God is our provider and that his promises and principles will hold true in our lives, we have the confidence to live our lives with a spirit of generosity and freedom. But it all comes down to where we have placed our faith. Is it anchored in ourselves, our job, or our circumstances, or is it firmly rooted in God?

To build a generous spirit, we have to make sure our faith is anchored in God and the principles we find in his Word.

Vision

The second thing we need to build a generous spirit is vision. Vision is simply a picture of a preferable future. Vision helps us see beyond where we are now to where we could be and want to be. It helps us look at opportunities, make decisions, avoid temptations, and manage our resources well. We need a picture for our lives that is in line with what God created us for, and that includes our finances. God wants us to be in a place of strength and health in every area of our lives so that we can be a blessing to others. We've already established the importance of building a generous spirit, but it won't happen on its own. We have to get a vision for it and be intentional.

In Philemon 1:6, we see that Paul hoped Philemon would get a vision for the great things that could be accomplished as a result of his generosity. Vision that's aligned with God's purpose keeps our lives from becoming just about us. We understand the incredible possibilities that can result from our generosity. Our lives aren't limited to pursuing our own desires and interests. Instead, we live for something much greater.

Godly vision causes us to live with an eternal perspective. We place more value on things that will matter for eternity rather than things that matter only here on earth. Only then can we really experience God's best for our lives and experience true significance.

First Timothy 6:18–19 says, "Command them to do good, to be rich in good deeds, and to be generous and willing to share. In this way they will lay up treasure for themselves as a firm foundation for the coming age, so that they may take hold of the life that is truly life." In his book *Mere Christianity*, C. S. Lewis put it this way: "If you read history you will find that the Christians who did most for the present world were precisely those who thought most of the next."[6]

Generosity lays a firm foundation for our lives. If we want our lives to make a lasting impact, we must live with vision and an eternal perspective. Kingdom principles and kingdom work are an investment that lasts forever.

Joy

Second Corinthians 9:7 says, "Each of you should give what you have decided in your heart to give, not reluctantly or under compulsion, for God loves a cheerful giver." The Amplified Version unpacks all the dimensions of the original language: "(He [God] takes pleasure in, prizes above other things, and is unwilling to abandon or to do without) a cheerful (joyous, 'prompt to do it') giver [whose heart is in his giving]."

The final ingredient we need for a generous spirit is joy. People with a generous spirit give joyfully and willingly. They are quick to give, and they give because they *want* to, not out of obligation or duty. The most generous people I know are addicted to giving to others. They just can't get enough of it. Joy in giving is a trademark of a generous spirit.

John D. Rockefeller said, "Think of giving not as a duty but as a privilege."[7] What an honor we have to be vehicles of God's blessing. Each time we are generous, we have the opportunity to bring God's love into someone's life in visible, tangible ways.

Cultivating these key ingredients of faith, vision, and joy will help us build and strengthen a generous spirit. Wherever we are on our journey to financial freedom, there is always room to expand our capacity to be generous. Even if doing so isn't easy, it's always worth it. Psalm 112:5 reminds us, "Good will come to those who are generous." Having a generous spirit expands our lives and positions us to experience true satisfaction and significance.

6

Blessed to Be a Blessing

Generosity is one of the core principles in the Bible for managing our finances, and a generous spirit brings tremendous benefits into our lives. But the greatest blessing of living with a generous spirit is the ability to make a difference in the lives of others. God wants to bless us and provide for us, but it's really about so much more.

God wants to provide for us so we can in turn help others. God never intended for us to keep his blessings all for ourselves. He created us to be conduits rather than reservoirs. His blessings flow *to* us so they can flow *through* us.

Second Corinthians 9:8 says, "And God is able to bless you abundantly, so that in all things at all times, having all that you need, you will abound in every good work." And 2 Corinthians 9:11 says, "You will be enriched in every way so that you can be generous on every occasion, and through us your generosity will result in thanksgiving to God."

These verses show us that God's provision and blessing are to enable us to lead generous lives. Notice the types of phrases Paul uses: "in all things," "at all times," "on every occasion." God intends for generosity to be a way of life for us. Opportunities for generosity are everywhere. God wants us to have the kind of spirit that is proactively looking for chances to be generous.

Isaiah 32:8 says, "But a generous man devises generous things, and by generosity he shall stand" (NKJV). The word *devises* has a connotation of strategy and planning, almost to the point of scheming. I love the picture that creates. Generous people are always scheming up ways to bless others. We have to make generosity a priority in our lives by building a generous spirit and then being intentional about creating opportunities to bless others. Where do we direct our generosity? The Bible indicates three specific areas.

1. Toward people
2. Toward the poor
3. Toward God's work

Generous toward People

Generosity isn't limited to our finances. It has much more to do with an attitude than an action. And one of the biggest ways that attitude comes into play in our lives is in our interactions with people. This may not be an area that comes to mind when we think about generosity, but it's one the Bible tells us is very important.

Colossians 3:13 says, "Make allowance for each other's faults, and forgive anyone who offends you. Remember, the Lord forgave you, so you must forgive others" (NLT). Having a generous spirit means we're full of grace and love toward other people. We're able to cut them a little slack and give them some room to be themselves, even allowing for mistakes. For you, making allowances might mean overlooking a grumpy comment at breakfast or picking up a wet towel that was left on the floor . . . again.

Sometimes having a generous spirit means releasing people from the pressure to measure up to our standards and simply loving them where they are, no strings attached. Being a harsh, controlling person who demands perfection is the opposite of how God wants us to treat people. Luke 6:37–38 says:

> Don't pick on people, jump on their failures, criticize their faults—unless, of course, you want the same treatment. Don't condemn those who are down; that hardness can boomerang. Be easy on people; you'll find life a lot easier. Give away your life; you'll find life given back, but not merely given back—given back with bonus and blessing. Giving, not getting, is the way. Generosity begets generosity. (Message)

The way we choose to treat the people in our lives determines what comes back to us. If you are constantly judgmental and critical of others, you probably find yourself living under a sense of condemnation. On the other hand, if you are quick to forgive and show grace to others, the same will be extended to you in an even greater measure.

Here are a few ways we can be generous toward people:

- with our forgiveness
- with our love
- with our words
- with our attitude
- with our patience
- with our time
- with our affection

Paul talked about his life being poured out like a drink offering for the people in whom he was investing (2 Tim. 4:6; Phil. 2:17). He chose not to hold anything back from the people in his world. We too need to make it a point to be generous in our attitude toward people. Don't go through life always keeping score and making people earn your goodwill and affection. Be willing to give freely of yourself and let good things flow out of your life into the lives of those around you. We all have far more to offer than just financial resources. Taking the time to offer a listening ear or a word of encouragement can be a powerful act of generosity.

Being generous toward people starts with understanding how generous God has been toward us. When we remember the forgiveness, the kindness, the patience, and the unconditional love God extends to us, we will want to do the same for others.

Generous toward the Poor

Throughout the Bible, God makes it clear that we are called to be generous toward those in need. Deuteronomy 15 gives us some important insight into this aspect of generosity:

> However, there need be no poor people among you, for in the land the LORD your God is giving you to possess as your inheritance, he will richly bless you, if only you fully obey the LORD your God and are careful to follow all these commands I am giving you today. (vv. 4–5)

> If anyone is poor among your fellow Israelites in any of the towns of the land the LORD your God is giving you, do not be hardhearted or tightfisted toward them. Rather, be openhanded and freely lend them whatever they need. (vv. 7–8)

> Give generously to them and do so without a grudging heart; then because of this the LORD your God will bless you in all your work and in everything you put your hand to. There will always be poor people in the land. Therefore I command you to be openhanded toward your fellow Israelites who are poor and needy in your land. (vv. 10–11)

This part of the Bible gives us a glimpse into God's heart and teaches us valuable lessons from the people of Israel. Many portions of the book of Deuteronomy were written as an instruction manual for Israel. To get the most out of these verses, we have to understand the context in which they were written.

The Israelites had been delivered from hundreds of years of slavery in Egypt, but they had not yet reached the Promised

Land. Before God brought the children of Israel into the Promised Land, he gave them some specific instructions on how they were to live when they got there. They had been slaves for so long that they didn't know how to operate in freedom. They weren't used to having their own land, owning their own homes, stewarding possessions, or managing their own lives. God wanted to set them up to win, so he laid out guidelines to help them navigate some of the issues they would face when they entered the land he was giving them.

The Bible calls the Old Testament "a shadow" of the New Testament. That term means the Old Testament is a glimpse of what's to come. First Corinthians tells us that everything that happened to the children of Israel happened as an example for us. I had three older sisters, and I found I could make my life a lot easier by watching and taking notes on what to do or, more often, what *not* to do. We can do the same thing when we read the Old Testament and learn from the children of Israel.

In the Bible, Egypt always represents a place of slavery or bondage. For us today, we could say it represents living beneath God's best for our lives (living contained or held back by something). For the children of Israel, the Promised Land held freedom, blessing, provision, and an incredible future. For you and me, the Promised Land is not a geographical location but rather living within God's best for us with those same benefits—freedom, blessing, provision, and a good plan for the future.

We can learn a lot from the instructions God gave the Israelites as they were approaching the Promised Land.

"There need be no poor people among you" (v. 4). First of all, God does not want anyone to be poor. Remember, for us today, the Promised Land represents God's best for our lives, and his best is that no one lives in poverty. While there will always be people in tough financial situations (Matt. 26:11), it's not what God wants, and we have the opportunity and the responsibility to help others through our generosity.

"He will richly bless you" (v. 4). The second thing we see is that God will richly bless us—not just bless us but richly bless us. However, there is a condition.

"If only you fully obey the LORD your God" (v. 5). The blessing comes when we fully obey God's instructions. Just as we saw with tithing, there's an if/then scenario that involves our part and God's part. *If* we obey, *then* God will bless us.

"Do not be hardhearted or tightfisted toward them. Rather, be openhanded and freely lend them whatever they need" (vv. 7–8). It's important that we recognize the significance of what God is saying here. He is speaking to his people and commissioning them to make sure they have the right attitude toward those who are poor. Notice that God doesn't tell the government to take care of the poor. He is telling *his people* to make sure they help those in need.

Today, "his people" refers to the church—you and me as part of the corporate body of believers. We are God's children, members of his body, and it is our responsibility to meet the needs of the poor in our cities and even beyond. We have to make sure we don't ever allow ourselves to have an attitude of disdain, frustration, or even complacency toward the poor.

God tells us not to be hardhearted toward them, withholding help and resources. Instead, we should be compassionate and do whatever we can to meet their needs. God makes it clear that a generous heart toward those in need is a key to receiving his blessings and promises in our own lives.

Just to make sure we get it, he emphasizes this again in verses 10 and 11 of Deuteronomy 15:

> Give generously to them [the poor] and do so without a grudging heart; then because of this the LORD your God will bless you in all your work and in everything you put your hand to. There will always be poor people in the land. Therefore I command you to be openhanded toward your fellow Israelites who are poor and needy in your land.

Notice that God doesn't just say "give." He says "give generously." I think this applies to both the amount we give and the spirit with which we give. As discussed in the last chapter, the Bible is clear that *how* we give is as important as *what* we give (2 Cor. 9:7).

This instruction was given in the strongest form possible, a command. Giving generously wasn't given as an option for the Israelites, and it's not an option for us today. If we want to experience God's best for our lives and carry out his plan here on earth, we can't turn a blind eye to those who are less fortunate or wait for someone else to take care of them.

Proverbs 21:13 says, "Those who shut their ears to the cries of the poor will be ignored in their own time of need" (NLT). Luke 12:48 tells us that to whom much is given much is required. Millions of people are struggling to meet their basic needs for food and shelter. No matter how much or how little we have, God has given it to us, not just for our provision and enjoyment but so that we can help others. In fact, the Bible tells us that whatever we do (or don't do) for "the least of these" we are actually doing for him (Matt. 25:40). How we treat the people that society considers least important is actually one of the greatest tests of our relationship with Jesus. Proverbs 19:17 says, "Whoever is kind to the poor lends to the LORD, and he will reward them for what they have done."

Many of us can relate to the situation the Israelites were in. We may not be in bondage anymore, but we aren't walking in the full promise God has for our lives, especially in the area of finances. Generosity was one of the keys God gave the Israelites to help them live out his best for their lives, and the same is true for us.

Generous toward God's Work

As believers, we've been given the mandate to take the gospel to the ends of the earth. This responsibility is both corporate and individual. Every believer has been called to make it a priority to help spread the message of the gospel. We may not all be called to go overseas as missionaries, but we can all invest our energy and resources into spreading the gospel. The word *gospel* simply means "good news." In a world that is filled with pain, searching, and hopelessness, we hold the best news possible: there is hope through Jesus Christ. Nothing is more important than helping people find a relationship with Jesus.

In Matthew 6:19–20, Jesus reminds us to keep our sights set on eternity as we go through life on this earth, saying,

"Don't store up treasures here on earth, where moths eat them and rust destroys them, and where thieves break in and steal. Store your treasures in heaven" (NLT). Paul talked about the "heavenly prize" he was focused on winning as he ran his race here on earth (Phil. 3:14).

Our material possessions and earthly achievements come to an end one day, but when people come to know Jesus, that is a reward that will last forever. If we focus only on today and achieving success in earthly terms, we'll miss out on what really matters for eternity.

Jim Elliot is an incredible example of someone who was focused on eternity. Elliot was an American missionary who was killed taking the gospel to an unreached tribe of people in Ecuador, the Auaca Indians. His journals record this saying several years before he was killed: "He is no fool who gives what he cannot keep to gain that which he cannot lose."[1]

Elliot understood that nothing on this earth holds greater value than reaching people for Jesus. He chose to devote his life to it, no matter what the cost. Few of us will ever be in a position to give our lives for the gospel, but we can willingly give of ourselves and our resources to move God's kingdom work forward on this earth. Nothing we invest in God's kingdom is ever wasted.

There are so many ways we can be generous toward kingdom work. I think of my good friends Pete and Kristi, who decided to drive an older car for another year so they could give more to our church's expansion initiatives. I remember Denzel, a teenager who sold cinnamon rolls and cookies every Wednesday to raise money so his friend Tim could go on a mission trip. I think of Lydia, who at sixteen didn't buy a car with her savings but rather used her savings to go to Africa to serve. I remember Kyle, who didn't take a promotion at work so he could keep serving a significant number of hours each week on the worship team at our church.

These are everyday people who honor God by being generous with their lives and their financial resources. We don't have to have a lot of money to honor God with it. Our attitude and what we do with our money matter to God. Being generous is about opening our hearts to God's purposes and making them a priority in our lives. As believers, we should have no greater passion than generously and wholeheartedly giving what we have to build, equip, and resource kingdom work, especially through our local church.

In Matthew 10:8, as Jesus is sending out his twelve disciples, he reminds them, "Give as freely as you have received!" (NLT). God didn't hold anything back from us. He gave his son Jesus to provide a way for us to find hope and freedom from sin. When we receive all the blessings that salvation and a relationship with Jesus bring, we also inherit a responsibility to go out and give others the opportunity to experience the same.

When we choose to have a generous spirit toward people, toward the poor, and toward God's work, we are acting in obedience to God's Word, which always positions us for blessing. The principle of generosity is one that has the power to make a huge impact on every area of our lives—emotionally, relationally, spiritually, as well as financially. Happiness and wealth don't always go together, but happiness and a generous spirit are almost inseparable. Amazing joy, freedom, and fulfillment come when we choose to live with a generous spirit.

The Secret of Contentment

So much could be said on the topic of finances. My goal in putting this book together was to provide a road map of practical steps taken directly from God's Word that will help us handle finances the best way—God's way.

We've covered three steps from God's Word that will position us for financial freedom. One more element found in the Bible is essential if we're going to follow God's instructions for our finances: contentment. This attitude has tremendous power in our lives, especially when it comes to finances.

The apostle Paul provides some great thoughts on living worry free in Philippians 4, which contains what may be the greatest passage on contentment in the Bible:

Not that I am implying that I was in any personal want, for I have learned how to be content (satisfied to the point where I am not disturbed or disquieted) in whatever state I am. I know how to be abased and live humbly in straitened circumstances, and I know also how to enjoy plenty and live in abundance. I have learned in any and all circumstances the secret of facing every situation, whether well-fed or going hungry, having a sufficiency and enough to spare or going without and being in want. I have strength for all things in Christ Who empowers me [I am ready for anything and equal to anything through Him Who infuses inner strength into me; I am self-sufficient in Christ's sufficiency]. (vv. 11–13 AMP)

I love Paul's definition of contentment: "satisfied to the point where I am not disturbed or disquieted." This is an incredible statement considering Paul was writing this letter from a prison cell. He had every reason to be frustrated, discouraged, and discontent, but instead, he chose contentment. He understood the power of contentment and its importance in a godly life.

This is a big issue for many of us. We can so quickly become unhappy with our life, and we end up going through it in a constant state of dissatisfaction. We're unhappy with our car, our house, our clothes, our job, our spouse, our opportunities, and the list goes on. More than anything, discontentment robs us of our ability to enjoy life. A lack of contentment prevents us from enjoying what God has given us—the people in our lives, the resources we have, and the opportunities before us. Ironically, the things we're dissatisfied with today are often what we were praying for not that long ago.

I'm not saying we shouldn't try to improve our lives or move forward. Contentment is not an attitude that causes us to sit back and not pursue progress or reach for greater things. In Philippians 3, just one chapter before Paul talks about contentment, he makes it clear that he's committed to constantly pressing forward. He says, "One thing I do: Forgetting what is behind and straining toward what is ahead, I press on" (vv. 13–14).

Paul was passionately committed to making progress, but he was also committed to not falling into the trap of frustration when challenges and setbacks came along. Sometimes in our pursuit of progress, we get discouraged and are tempted to resign ourselves to just accept where we are.

We have to remember that God intends for both pursuit of progress and contentment to be at work in our lives at the same time. We can choose to value and appreciate all the good things we have right now while still holding on to that picture of a preferable future.

Paul put it this way in 1 Timothy 6:6: "Godliness with contentment is great gain." Contentment by itself can lead to complacency. We have to add godliness to it, which means we're pursuing the things of God. When we pursue God and godly goals and ambitions, and we pair that with a commitment not to be anxious or to lose our peace on the way, that's when we experience great gain.

Let's look at three key thoughts Paul teaches about contentment.

Contentment Is Learned

In Philippians 4:11, Paul says, "I have *learned* how to be content" (AMP, emphasis mine). Paul didn't always know

91

how to be content; it was something he had to work on. Contentment isn't something most of us have naturally. We have to teach ourselves how to be content. Contentment is a mark of spiritual maturity. When we can be happy with where we are and what we have, even though we hope for more, that's maturity.

We've talked several times about the importance of having a vision for our lives and our finances. But we can't ever let that vision create frustration, discouragement, and unhealthy dissatisfaction with where we currently are. If we're not careful, that frustration can get into our spirits and steal our peace.

The Bible talks about a special rest that God wants for his people (Heb. 4:9). This rest isn't like taking a week off and not doing anything. This kind of rest is an inner peace, an assurance that comes from trusting in God's power and strength. Living in a constant state of frustration is not healthy, enjoyable, or God's desire for us. We have to guard our hearts and learn to be content so that our vision for a better future doesn't steal our rest right now.

Contentment is not a one-time experience or achievement. It doesn't come into our lives through a divine impartation or a single encounter with God's presence. Contentment is a learned skill that we must cultivate in ourselves and practice daily. It doesn't matter what our personality type is. Even though some people are naturally more inclined toward being content (or discontent), the truth is that contentment is a character issue and a spiritual discipline we're all responsible to develop, regardless of our personality.

The apostle Paul was a driven, ambitious man. Before his encounter with Jesus on the Damascus road, Paul was on a religious mission to kill Christians. He was a type A, whatever-it-takes-to-win kind of person. His personality would hardly be conducive to contentment and satisfaction. Yet he wrote the greatest insight on contentment—while he was confined to prison in chains, no less. As with Paul, God's power at work within us gives us the ability to live with a sense of contentment in our hearts.

Contentment Gives Us the Know-how to Deal with Life's Ups and Downs

Paul is sharing with us "the secret of facing every situation" (Phil. 4:12 AMP). Paul understood how to be content when he didn't have all he needed or wanted. But on the other hand, Paul also understood how to exercise contentment and enjoy life when he had more than enough.

Contentment isn't just for situations when our resources come up short. We have to learn how to be content when we get some momentum in our finances and abundance flows into our lives. Some people, even when they have more than enough, still aren't satisfied, and they aren't able to enjoy it. Benjamin Franklin said, "Content makes poor men rich; discontent makes rich men poor."[1] One of the most important skills we can develop is to be satisfied and enjoy what we have, no matter how little or how much it may be.

The reality is that, whether we like it or not, we all face ups and downs in life. Sometimes things go our way, and sometimes they don't. When we build contentment into our lives, we have the know-how and the strength to deal successfully with both the good and the bad so we can keep moving forward.

Here are some contentment know-hows we need to have.

Know how to walk by faith and trust God. The only way we really learn how to walk by faith is by facing situations we can't handle on our own. I remember when Leslie and I went on the mission field in Africa. Raising the funds we needed to get there, the whole process of moving overseas, and all the situations we faced once we arrived gave us plenty of opportunities to practice trusting God.

I'll never forget one particular incident while we were there. The economy in Kenya collapsed, and the shilling devalued significantly. As a result, our expenses literally tripled overnight. We'd been operating with just enough support funds for what we needed. When the economy collapsed, we didn't know how we were going to cover the extra costs. It was a very serious situation for a lot of people, and many missionaries moved home. We decided to stay in Kenya and trust God to provide. Sure enough, our monthly financial support went up just enough. For three months during the economic upheaval, it stayed there, and as soon as everything went back to normal, it went right back to where it had been before. God knew exactly what we needed to get us through.

Hebrews 12 tells us that what can be shaken will be shaken. When things in our world start to shake, we have to reach down deep and remember we are citizens of "an unshakable kingdom." We don't place our trust in a person or a relationship, in our job, in our government, or in anything else to provide for us. We give respect and honor where it's due and pray for our authorities to make good decisions, but at the end of the day, we place our trust in God above all else.

Know how to stay positive and happy when we face challenges. Philippians 2:14 says, "Do all things without grumbling and faultfinding and complaining [against God] and questioning and doubting [among yourselves]" (AMP).

This is so much easier said than done! Sometimes we don't even realize we're complaining. I encourage you to try this exercise. Try to go an entire day without complaining or grumbling. It can be a challenge. But this is actually how God wants us to live every day. When we learn to be content, we have the ability to keep our spirits up and our outlook positive, even when we may not like how things are going. There is always something to be happy and thankful for, if we're willing to keep our perspective right.

Our feelings and emotions can be powerful things, but we don't have to allow them to dictate our lives or rob us of joy. Sometimes we have to step in and speak to our soul, just as the psalmist did in Psalm 42:11: "Why, my soul, are you downcast? Why so disturbed within me? Put your hope in God, for I will yet praise him, my Savior and my God."

When we're tempted to be unhappy or negative about our circumstances, we need to take charge of our thoughts and feelings. Complaining about our situations and our finances won't change anything. In fact, complaining usually discourages us more. We need to choose to focus on the blessings we *do* have rather than what we *don't* have.

Know how to keep the vision in sight when there's resistance. Maybe your goal or vision is to pay off debt. But then the brakes go out on your car. And then you find out there won't be any holiday bonuses this year. What do you do in that situation? Do you throw your vision out the window and give up on getting out of debt? No. When we have a vision for something that pleases God and benefits our lives, we need to hold on to it in spite of resistance. We may have to make some adjustments, but we shouldn't abandon the vision when things get tough. Being content helps us not to get impatient during seasons of delay. We have to remember that delay is not denial.

Nehemiah is a great example of someone in the Bible who had a vision to do something significant and faced a lot of resistance when trying to accomplish it. It was in his heart to repair the wall of Jerusalem, which had been broken down and neglected for many years. He made a plan and started rebuilding the wall, but he faced many challenges along the way. People mocked him, got angry with him, and even plotted to harm him. So what did Nehemiah do? He strapped on a sword and went back to work (Neh. 4:16–18). He didn't get discouraged and give up. He pressed through the resistance and continued to do what he knew was right. And, amazingly enough, he and the other workers completed the wall in just fifty-two days.

As a Christian, anytime you're trying to improve your life or do something significant, you *will* encounter resistance. Resistance can come in a variety of ways—negative people, difficult circumstances, plans that don't work out. Challenges can cause you to want to pull back and rethink your vision or wonder if it's too hard. Press through those seasons. Stay committed to the principles in God's Word and the process of handling things God's way. Contentment helps us not to give up before the vision is accomplished.

Contentment Doesn't Come from Without; It Comes from Within

We can't rely on external things to bring us contentment. That's why Paul says, "I have strength for all things in Christ Who empowers me [I am ready for anything and equal to anything through Him Who infuses *inner* strength into me; I am self-sufficient in Christ's sufficiency]" (Phil. 4:13 AMP, emphasis mine).

One of the biggest misconceptions in our world today is that our circumstances determine our contentment. People think, "If I just had . . . ," and then they rattle off a list of things they think would bring them satisfaction and fulfillment. But if that were true, we wouldn't see so many people who seem to have it all and yet are still so empty inside.

Contentment doesn't come when our circumstances change. Contentment comes when we make changes on the inside. We find true satisfaction when we make the choice to be happy right where we are. I love Joyce Meyer's wise advice: "Enjoy where you are on the way to where you are going."[2]

Contentment may not be the most exciting piece of the puzzle when it comes to managing money, but it's part of what it takes to experience God's best. A heart that has learned the secret of godly contentment can go the distance with peace and joy, no matter what happens along the way. Contentment is one of the keys to seeing God's promises come to pass in our lives.

Conclusion

When it comes to following God's prescription for our finances, we could sum it up with the title of the famous hymn "Trust and Obey." The chorus of this timeless song by John H. Sammis gives us a simple yet powerful reminder of how we find true peace and happiness on our journey with God.

> Trust and obey, for there's no other way
> To be happy in Jesus, but to trust and obey.

Virtually every principle we find in God's Word that leads us toward God's best requires these two things of us: trust and obedience. The steps of tithing consistently, managing our finances wisely, and building a generous spirit are no different. They require us to trust the principle God has given and then obey it by putting it into practice in our lives.

Trust and obedience naturally occur together. If we don't have both activated in our lives, we won't be able to unlock the full benefits of God's promises. Trust and obedience work together to lead us toward a life of peace that's free of worry and anxiety.

It's not always easy to trust, and it's not always easy to obey—especially when our circumstances are challenging, when we don't have all the answers, or when we would choose to do things another way. But there is one thing we can always go back to when our faith is tested: God's faithfulness. It's one of the greatest sources of strength and peace for our lives. Remembering God's faithfulness to his promises makes it easier to trust and obey him. Psalm 145:13 says, "The LORD is trustworthy in all he promises and faithful in all he does." We can be confident that God keeps his word.

To receive the full benefits of God's promises, we first have to do our part and follow the instructions given in his Word. I want to encourage you to do your part—and to start doing it right away. Remember the three steps discussed in this book:

1. Tithe consistently by giving the first 10 percent of your income to God through your local church.

2. Manage the money God gives you wisely.

3. Build a generous spirit in your heart and mind.

Don't put off taking these steps or wait for a more "ideal" time. The Bible tells us that if we wait for perfect conditions, we'll never get anything done (Eccles. 11:4 NLT). The time to start is now. A big part of obedience is simply making a choice and then following through. Real obedience means obeying all the way, right away. Partial or delayed obedience really isn't obedience at all. The benefits and blessings come when we obey fully and don't drag our feet or try to get around our responsibilities. The kind of obedience that is pleasing to God comes from a submitted, soft heart that wants to please God above all else. When we have that kind of heart, we bring God's favor into our lives.

Here are three simple thoughts to encourage you on your journey to worry-free finances.

1. *Start small.* Zechariah 4:10 tells us, "Do not despise these small beginnings, for the LORD rejoices to see the work begin" (NLT). Sometimes it can feel overwhelming to try to make a change, but something is better than nothing! Don't underestimate the power of making small changes. Sometimes the "smallest" changes can bring big results.

2. *Expect the best.* No matter what your current situation is right now, know that God's power and his presence are available to help you. Choose to look at your future with faith and positive expectations. Things *can* change, and your future *can* be different. You're not in this alone. God's given you his Word to guide you, and he'll be with you every step of the way.

3. *Don't give up.* Galatians 6:9 reminds us, "Let us not become weary in doing good, for at the proper time we will reap a harvest if we do not give up." As you follow the steps in this book and practice contentment, your life will reap the benefits. I know it won't always be easy, and things probably won't change overnight, but stay committed to the process. God's principles produce results. If you're faithful to do your part, he'll be faithful to do his.

Nothing can compare to the feeling of knowing we have anchored our trust in an unchanging, unshakable God and that we've done our part to obey all he's asked of us. We will experience peace and joy that we can't get anywhere else. When we trust and obey, we can live worry free.

Budget Guide

Here are some basic budget categories and average percentages to serve as a guideline as you establish a budget. The percentages listed represent the amount of your spendable income that goes toward that category.

To calculate your spendable income, add up your total income each month and deduct your monthly tithe, taxes, and money to establish a $1,000 emergency fund if you do not have one. Once you have established your $1,000 emergency fund, you no longer need to take this money out of your total income at the beginning of each month, but it is wise to continue to save.

Total income:	$ _____
Tithe (10%):	$ _____
Taxes:	$ _____
Emergency Fund:	$ _____
Spendable Income:	$ _____

Once you know the amount of your spendable income, apply the following percentages to come up with a basic guideline for your monthly budget. (Note: It's important that you account for the different costs that fall under each category. For example, your transportation category needs to account for more than just your car payment; you have to take into consideration your car insurance, gas, repairs, and yearly fees for taxes and tags.)

Housing—32%	$ _____
Food and groceries—15%	$ _____
Transportation—15%	$ _____
Life insurance—2%	$ _____
Clothing—5%	$ _____
Debts—5%	$ _____
Savings—5%	$ _____
Medical—7%	$ _____
Gifts—2%	$ _____
Entertainment/recreation—7%	$ _____
Miscellaneous—5%	$ _____

These percentages are recommendations to help you get started. Each person or family is different, and you can adjust the percentages as needed to fit your particular needs. But remember, if you increase one category's percentage, you've got to compensate by lowering another. The bottom line in successful budgeting is that your total percentages always add up to 100 percent.

For additional resources, I recommend the following:

Blue, Ron. *Master Your Money: A Step-by-Step Plan for Financial Freedom*. Nashville: Thomas Nelson, 1997.

Crown Financial Ministries, www.crown.org

Ramsey, Dave. *Financial Peace*. New York: Viking, 1997.

Notes

Introduction

1. www.Merriam-Webster.com/dictionary/worry, accessed October 24, 2012.

2. W. E. Vine, John R. Kohlenberger, and James A. Swanson, *The Expanded Vine's Expository Dictionary of New Testament Words* (Minneapolis: Bethany, 1984), s.v. "eleutheros."

3. *Webster's New World College Dictionary* (Cleveland: Wiley Publishing, 2010), s.v. "free."

4. Ibid.

5. Ibid.

6. Brian Tracy, *Maximum Achievement: Strategies and Skills That Will Unlock Your Hidden Powers to Succeed* (New York: Fireside, 1995), 28.

7. David Bach, *Start Late, Finish Rich: A No-Fail Plan for Achieving Financial Freedom at Any Age* (New York: Broadway Books, 2006), 7.

8. Federal Reserve, www.federalreserve.gov/releases/g/9/, accessed June 12, 2013.

9. United States Courts, www.uscourts.gov, November 7, 2012, accessed June 12, 2013.

10. Danny Kofke, "One in Four Americans Would Not Inform Spouse of Financial Difficulties," *Marriage and Money: Communicating about Financial Difficulties*, www.onemoneydesign.com/one-in-four-americans-would-not-inform-spouse-of-financial-difficulties, October 25, 2011, accessed September 18, 2012.

Chapter 1: Laying the Foundation for Worry-Free Finances

1. Merriam-Webster, www.merriam-webster.com/dictionary/tithe, accessed September 17, 2012.

2. William Green, "The Secrets of John Templeton," *Money*, January 1, 1999, www.CNNMoney.com, accessed October 30, 2012.

3. Matthew Kirdahy, "Templeton Saw It Coming," July 8, 2008, www.Forbes.com, accessed October 30, 2012.

4. "50 Most Generous Philanthropists," www.Businessweek.com, accessed October 30, 2012.

5. Green, "Secrets of John Templeton."

6. Ibid.

7. Hansen, Mark Victor and Robert G. Allen, *The One Minute Millionaire: The Enlightened Way to Wealth* (New York: Three Rivers, 2009), 84.

8. www.presbyterianendowment.org, accessed June 13, 2013.

Chapter 2: The Power of the First Part

1. Borger, Justin, "Love and Money," GenerousGiving.org, accessed June 13, 2013.

2. Oswald Chambers and James Reimann, *My Utmost for His Highest* (Grand Rapids: Discovery House, 2006), 6.

3. Ron Blue, *Master Your Money* (Nashville: Thomas Nelson, 1997).

Chapter 3: Planning for Success

1. www.ziglar.com/quotes/zig-ziglar/if-you-aim-nothing, accessed June 11, 2013.

2. Dickler, Jessica, "Most Americans Can't Afford $1,000 Emergency Expense," *CNN Money*, August 11, 2011, www.money.cnn.com/2011/08/10/pf/emergency_fund/index.htm, accessed June 11, 2013.

3. Buschman, Kathryn Vasal, "Why We Overspend," *Fox Business*, June 1, 2011, www.foxbusiness.com, accessed June 11, 2013.

4. Janet Novack, "Credit Card Debt Blamed for Surge in Elder Bankruptcy," October 12, 2010, www.Forbes.com, accessed September 17, 2012.

5. Ramsey, Dave and Sharon Ramsey, *Financial Peace Revisited* (New York: Viking, 2003), 297.

Chapter 4: Developing Good Habits

1. www.dictionary.com/browse/diligence, accessed June 12, 2013.

2. *Webster's Revised Unabridged Dictionary* (Springfield, MA: C & G Merriam, 1913), s.v. "diligence."

3. "Character First—Diligence," *Character First—Diligence*, Character Training Institute, www.qcinspect.com/article/diligence.htm, accessed November 6, 2012.

4. Atul Gawande, "Personal Best," *New Yorker*, October 3, 2011, www.newyorker.com, accessed November 6, 2012.

5. ESPN Staff, "The Wizard's Wisdom: 'Woodenisms,'" June 4, 2010, www.ESPN.com, accessed November 6, 2012.

6. Matthew Easton, *Illustrated Bible Dictionary*, 3rd ed. (Nashville: Thomas Nelson, 1897), s.v. "faithful."

Chapter 5: The Foundation of a Generous Spirit

1. www.thefreedictionary.com/generous, accessed November 9, 2012.

2. www.Merriam-Webster.com/dictionary/generous, accessed November 9, 2012.

3. www.Merriam-Webster.com/dictionary/spirit, accessed November 7, 2012.

4. www.Biblegateway.com, accessed November 10, 2012.

5. Lisa Firestone, "Generosity—What's in It for You?" November 24, 2010, www.PsychologyToday.com, accessed November 9, 2012.

6. C. S. Lewis, *Mere Christianity* (San Francisco: HarperSanFrancisco, 2001), 135.

7. Keith Hinkle, "The Joy and Impact of Giving," *Pepperdine Magazine*, April 19, 2010, Pepperdine University, www.magazine.pepperdine.edu, accessed November 7, 2012.

Chapter 6: Blessed to Be a Blessing

1. Elisabeth Elliot, *Shadow of the Almighty: The Life and Testament of Jim Elliot* (New York: Harper, 1958), 15.

Chapter 7: The Secret of Contentment

1. Benjamin Franklin, *Poor Richard's Almanack* (Waterloo, IA: U.S.C., 1914), 18.

2. Joyce Meyer, *Enjoying Where You Are on the Way to Where You Are Going: Learning How to Live a Joyful Spirit-led Life* (Tulsa: Harrison House, 1996).

John Siebeling is lead pastor of The Life Church, a thriving, ethnically diverse 7,000-member multi-campus church in Memphis, Tennessee. He is a member of the Board of Directors for ARC (Association of Related Churches) and is a widely respected peer of other well-known ARC pastors. The Life Church has a weekly television program with over 125,000 viewers on average weekly. John has twenty plus years of ministry experience, including several years serving alongside his wife as missionaries to Kenya.